The Ramsgate T Railwa

GW00393452

Peter A. Harding

A two car yellow train waits for passengers at Hereson Road Station on July 25th 1958. This two car train was half of a four car yellow train that was originally supplied new when the line opened and which could be split to run as two independent two car trains.

Alan A. Jackson

Published by

Peter A. Harding

"Mossgiel", Bagshot Road, Knaphill,
Woking, Surrey GU21 2SG.

ISBN 0 9523458 9 7

Contents

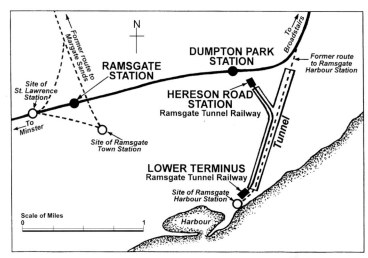

A two car yellow train at the lower terminus on September 9th 1964. This station appears never to have had an official name and was at various times referred to as either 'Sands', 'Beach' or 'Olympia'.

H.C.Casserley

Introduction

The Ramsgate Tunnel Railway was unique in that it not only ran its full length (apart from its two stations) in a tunnel, but also for the fact that it was a 2ft gauge line worked by an overhead electric cable in tramway style.

To give passengers something to look at while in the tunnel, it had when opened, illuminated scenes on the tunnel walls which depicted views from around the world. Because of this, the railway was known as "The World Scenic Railway".

Although it was seen as something of a novelty, the line served a real purpose by linking the amusement park on the beach known as "Merrie England" with the Dumpton Park area of Ramsgate at Hereson Road which was not only close to Dumpton Park Station on the main line between Broadstairs and Ramsgate, but also the Greyhound Stadium.

The tunnel was originally used by main line standard gauge trains to a station at Ramsgate Harbour which opened in 1863 but, in 1926 when the Southern Railway decided to rearrange the railway setup in the Ramsgate area they closed the line from south of Broadstairs to Ramsgate Harbour leaving the tunnel and station abandoned and the track lifted.

When the Ramsgate Tunnel Railway came into being in 1936, it only used two thirds of the original tunnel from the southern end to a new smaller tunnel which was excavated inland from the original tunnel to come to the surface at Bradshaw's field near Hereson Road. This new tunnel was much smaller in dimensions being 8ft high and 6ft wide.

I hope that this publication reminds local people and railway enthusiasts of this interesting little enterprise from a bygone era.

A two car red train at Hereson Road Station on July 5th 1953. Like their yellow counterparts, the two car red trains were also half of a four car red train supplied new for the opening of the line.   John H. Meredith

Railways come to Ramsgate

The Kentish seaside town of Ramsgate was first reached by rail when the South Eastern Railway (SER) opened their line from Ashford via Canterbury on April 13th 1846 with a station originally called Ramsgate but later called Ramsgate Town. It was situated at the back of the town, about a mile from the sea front. The line was then extended north across the Isle of Thanet to Margate Sands on December 1st 1846. Seventeen years later, on October 5th 1863, the Kent Coast Railway opened their extension from Herne Bay via Birchington, Margate and Broadstairs with a terminus at Ramsgate in a very favourable position alongside the beach near the pier and harbour. The line was worked from the outset by the London Chatham & Dover Railway (LC&DR) who absorbed the Kent Coast Railway on July 13th 1871. The new terminus was originally opened as Ramsgate (C&D) but was soon changed to Ramsgate Harbour Station. It was situated just below a cliff and was approached through a 1,124 yard tunnel on a 1 in 75 down gradient.

Although well appointed with four platforms, a turntable and sidings, the whole area was rather cramped and down trains needed a cautious approach through the tunnel with its steep gradient while up trains experienced a difficult standing start. Even so, the LC&DR no doubt felt very pleased to have gained "one up" on their great rivals the SER.

The two companies spent much time and money trying to "out do" each other throughout Kent during this period, which often resulted in towns like Ramsgate and Margate unnecessarily being supported by two separate railway companies.

Although this situation was not ideal, things stayed that way even after 1898 when the two companies agreed to work together but remain independent under the heading of the South Eastern & Chatham Railway Management Committee (SE&CR).

Ramsgate Harbour Station with the sands in the foreground.

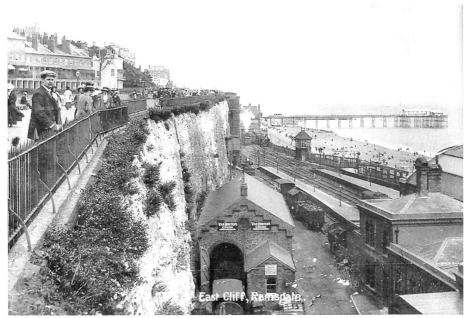

Looking down at the station from the East Cliff Promenade. The iron built Marina Pier which was demolished in 1930 can be seen in background.   Lens of Sutton

View of the tunnel from the platform at Ramsgate Harbour Station.   Denis Cullum Collection

This view with the tide in, shows just how cramped the whole station area really was.

The SE&CR no doubt considered the duplication of lines at Ramsgate and Margate was not ideal but, it was not until the Railway Grouping of 1923 when the SE&CR became part of the newly formed Southern Railway that any positive action was taken.

The Southern Railway quickly decided that the best plan would be to link the former LC&DR line from a point just north of the tunnel leading to Ramsgate Harbour Station with the former SER line near Ramsgate Town Station. A new main Ramsgate Station would be built nearby the existing Ramsgate Town Station (although slightly further away from the sea) and also a new station would be built at Dumpton Park, a north-east suburb of Ramsgate.

Looking at the station from the sidings which were next to the tunnel, to the right of the photograph.

The new link line was completed and opened to the public on July 2nd 1926 and from this date the former SER line between Ramsgate Town and Margate Sands stations was closed as well as both stations. The former LC&DR line through the tunnel and Ramsgate Harbour Station also closed at the same time.

With all these changes happening, it now meant that the disused line running through the tunnel and the disused station on the sea front were available for alternative use.

The former station building was acquired by Thanet Amusements Limited who using the name "Merrie England" established a fun-fair, small zoo and refreshment facilities.

By 1933, "Merrie England" was becoming very popular and Ramsgate Olympia Ltd., was founded as a private company to take over the running of the enterprise from Thanet Amusements Ltd. The new company decided that the disused tunnel which had been sealed up after the track was removed should now be put to good use.

A train heads towards Ramsgate Harbour Station via the tunnel, while on the right, the new line curving to Dumpton Park and Ramsgate is under construction.   Southern Railway Magazine

After the new line to Ramsgate was completed and the track through the tunnel removed.
Railway Magazine

The Tunnel Railway

After much thought, and several suggestions, Mr.D.F.Warren the managing director of Ramsgate Olympia Ltd., who seems to have been the driving force behind any schemes for the possible use of the tunnel, approached the Southern Railway with an idea which was referred to as the 1933 scheme. The suggestion was to re-lay the track through the tunnel and to build yet another new station between Broadstairs and Ramsgate. As it would have meant three stations on just a mile of track, the Southern Railway felt that it would be impracticable and would have been far to costly.

Not to be out done by this, Mr. Warren approached the Ramsgate Council in 1934 with another scheme but, as with the previous idea, this was also turned down.

The company finally decided that some form of 'light' rail connection via the tunnel would provide a good link with the Dumpton Park area where the greyhound track was proving very popular plus also providing a service with Dumpton Park Station.

The idea was for a new 2ft gauge track to use all the tunnel from the beach apart from the last 344 yards from the top exit. From this point a new tunnel needed to be excavated inland to come to the surface at Bradshaw's field where a new terminus would be built with an entrance at Hereson Road at the back of gardens from the adjoining end of Muir Road, just a few minutes walk from Dumpton Park Station. This new scheme met with all round approval.

The new tunnel would not be like the original tunnel but would have smaller dimensions being just 8ft high and 6ft wide and on a 1 in 15 gradient. The whole length of the line from the beach to Hereson Road would be 1,144 yards.

Although various forms of motive power were discussed, ranging from rope haulage to mechanical traction, it was finally decided to use electric operation with an overhead tram style cable.

As an added attraction, another idea for a journey which was in a tunnel throughout, was to have colourful illuminated tableaux depicting scenes from various foreign locations on the wall of part of the original tunnel. This innovation was to lead to the line becoming known as "The World Scenic Railway".

The former Ramsgate Harbour Station building in 1932 under its new name of "Merrie England".

Author's Collection

To organise the construction and operation of the new line, Ramsgate Olympia Ltd., set up a wholly-owned subsidiary called Tunnel Railway Ltd., with Mr.D.A.I.Muntz (an associate of Mr.D.F.Warren) as managing director.

The main contractor appointed to construct the line and new tunnel was the Holborn Construction Co. Ltd., of Holborn Viaduct, London EC1 who were well known in the area having recently completed work on the Winterstoke undercliff. Work started in May of 1936 and they were given just three months to complete everything with the hope of opening for the August Bank Holiday weekend..

Holborn Construction Co. Ltd., in turn placed the contract for the rolling stock and the electrical sub-station with English Electric Co. Ltd. The rolling stock consisted of two four car trains, which were constructed at their Preston site.

The station building at Hereson Road was designed by Mr. Wood of Birmingham based architects Messrs. Wood, Kendrick and Reynolds and built by Messrs. Darby and Martin of Ramsgate.

The consulting engineer was Henry Greenly who was a pioneer of miniature passenger carrying railways. Having started in 1897 as a draughtsman at the Neasden Works of the Metropolitan Railway under James Hunter, the chief draughtsman, he went on to work for many years with W.J.Bassett Lowke designing locomotives for miniature railways in Britain and abroad as well as involvement with various model railway magazines. In 1911 he designed the route, buildings, locomotives and rolling stock for the Rhyl Miniature Railway, while in 1922 he became engineer to the Ravenglass & Eskdale Railway which, under his guidance, was converted to 15in gauge. He was mainly known for his association with the Romney, Hythe & Dymchurch 15in gauge line where he was responsible for all civil engineering, and the design of locomotives and rolling stock from the line's inception in 1926 until its completion in 1930.

Henry Greenly
(1876 - 1947)
Author's Collection

The fun-fair at the "Merrie England" site.

Railway Magazine

Holborn Construction Co. Ltd., wasted no time in getting things moving and the 'first sod' was cut by Miss Jean Warren, daughter of Mr.D.F.Warren on May 2nd 1936 at the Hereson Road Station site.

Miss Jean Warren turning the first sod at the Hereson Road Station site on May 2nd 1936. Behind her are seen (left to right) Mr. Muirhead (resident manager of Holborn Construction), Mr.D.A.I.Muntz (of the Tunnel Railway Ltd), Mrs. Muntz, Mrs. Warren, Mr.D.F.Warren (managing director of Ramsgate Olympia Ltd.), and Mr. Bill Cooper (general foreman of the construction works). Standing on the mechanical excavator is Paddy Warren, son of Mr.D.F.Warren.

East Kent Times

The *East Kent Times* reported the following in their May 6th 1936 issue:-

Work is proceeding apace on Ramgate's new underground railway, which is to connect the Hereson district with the promenade. In order to complete the task by the allotted date, workmen are engaged day and night.

Driving the new tunnel in progress from the Hereson Road Station site.   East Kent Times

A group of men engaged in the construction of the new tunnel.   East Kent Times

With work progressing well, Mr.D.F.Warren was able to address the Ramsgate Chamber of Commerce and inform them of how well things were going. This meeting was reported in the *East Kent Times* in their June 13th 1936 issue as follows:-

ROUND THE WORLD IN FIVE MINUTES!
ON RAMSGATE'S UNDERGROUND RAILWAY
MR.D.F.WARREN'S DREAMS OF THE FUTURE

Nothing envisaged of Jules Verne transcends the concrete schemes and more ephemeral dreams of Mr.D.F.Warren, managing director of Ramsgate Olympia Ltd.

As is generally known, Mr. Warren's company recently commenced its latest venture – the construction of the underground railway from Bradshaw's field near Dumpton Park Station to the old Harbour Station site now occupied by "Merrie England".

On Tuesday morning, Mr. Warren addressed the members of the Ramsgate Chamber of Commerce on the new scheme and its future development.

After tracing the negotiations which led up to the commencement of the driving of the tunnel, Mr. Warren revealed that the scenic decorations for the new mode of transport were being carried out by the man who is responsible for most of C.B.Cockrane's stage decorations.

Starting from Ramsgate Harbour the traveller would be taken, he said, to New York, down to South America, across the Pacific to South Africa, through the jungle to Asia and back to Ramsgate – all in the space of five minutes!

Mr. Warren also revealed plans of his, which he styled "dreams and castles in the air", for the development of the underground railway at Ramsgate and district serving the district of Newington and the airport.

Future Developments

Speaking with regard to the future development of the land he had acquired at Hereson, Mr. Warren said that a certain amount of space had been reserved for a housing estate on the Dumpton Park drive side of the site. It was also intended to build a very large charabanc car park. Further, there was another scheme which some people might consider a dream and others a nightmare, to build a Stadium capable of seating 10,000 people.

"If we build a place of that size and can get the people there", said Mr. Warren, "we can afford to pay a very large sum for the programme, and if we pay a large sum for the programme, I believe, and it seems only common sense, that we shall get the people. What sort of shows there would be I cannot say at the moment. Personally, I think professional tennis might be one big attraction".

Dealing more fully with the Ramsgate district railway scheme, Mr. Warren pointed out that with the trams done away with, it was going to be rather difficult to carry about four million over the district every year on the surface. There was air travel it was true, but underground seemed an even more reasonable method of carrying the traffic.

Electric Trains

Mr. Warren then produced plans of the type of electric train he proposed to use on the portion of underground railway now under construction. It would be noticed, he said, that overhead wire had been favoured. The third rail on the ground had been considered, but it had to be remembered that the railway would carry a large number of children and that the overhead wire would undoubtedly prove more safe.

The old tunnel, continued the speaker had been inspected by a representative of the Ministry of Transport, and had been found to be in perfect condition. The gradient of the old tunnel was 1 in 75, and the gradient of the new tunnel, which would have concrete walls three feet thick, would be 1 in 15. The trains would be equipped with three types of brake and the "dead man's handle" employed on the London Underground, so that the margin of safety would be very large.

The railway would be 1,300 yards long and with two trains which would be used to start with the capacity would be 1,000 passengers each way per hour.

Ramsgate's Potentialities

In the course of his address Mr. Warren said he believed Ramsgate was a town which had never realised its potentialities of aspect and character and which had allowed itself to fall behind its neighbours. At present many people, not relishing the long and tedious walk from the Ramsgate Town Station to the sands, alighted either at Margate or Broadstairs, where conditions were more favourable. By the new scheme the day-tripper, for whom it was intended the railway should exclusively cater, would be able to spend nearly an hour longer in Ramsgate.

At the conclusion of his address the chairman (Mr. Walter Daniel) expressed thanks to the speaker for an interesting and absorbing address. Mr. Warren had shown them, he said, that the day tripper could get almost straight from the station to the sands, the results must be advantageous to Ramsgate. It could not be said that the new railway would make much difference to the traders because not many years ago, visitors were taken straight to Ramsgate Harbour Station.

The vote of thanks was seconded by Mr. A.J.H. Taylor and carried unanimously.

The Hereson Road Station site under construction.
Author's Collection

While things were progressing well on the site of the new railway, English Electric Co. Ltd., were constructing the electric trains at their works at Preston. The order was for two, four car trains which looked very similar but were in fact slightly different. One was painted red and lined in yellow while the other one was yellow with blue lining. The yellow train was capable of splitting into two separate two car trains. The intention for this was that during peak times when the line was busy, both four car trains could be used but, when things were slack the two halves of the yellow train could handle the service.

The red, four car train consisted of a motor car at each end and two trailer cars in the centre. The motor cars were 25ft 6ins long while the trailer cars were 21ft 9ins making the train an overall length of 94ft 6ins. The cars were 4ft 4ins wide and were 7ft 6ins from the rail to the top of the roof. The yellow train also had a motor car at each end, but the two centre cars were driving trailers for when the train was split. These two trailer cars were both 2ft 6ins longer than the red train trailer cars to accommodate the extra driving positions, making the overall length of the yellow train to 99ft 6ins.

Each four car train had a motor at each end which was in fact, a heavy power bogie to which the adjacent car was articulated, with a specially designed bogie at the other end. The centre cars had similar bogies. The driving position was immediately behind each power bogie on the frame of the first car and separated from the seating area by a glass partitioned bulkhead. Each train weighed 21 tons unladen and was capable of seating 108 passengers which comprised of 24 in the motor cars and 30 in each of the trailer cars. The cars were open at the sides with double cross-bench seats with fixed backs which seated three passengers abreast.

As it was later found that the service could normally be handled by the two car yellow trains, the four car red train was modified to also operate in two parts. To do this, a driving position in the two centre cars was created very much like the yellow train, which meant a loss of three seats in each car.

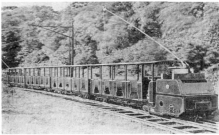

(*Above*) The four car red train at the English Electric works at Preston. The special length trolley pole was for use on the multi-gauge test track.
GEC Traction Ltd

(*Left*) The four car yellow and red trains at Hereson Road Station prior to the line opening.
GEC Traction Ltd

Testing a two car yellow train at Hereson Road Station just before the line opened.
Pleasurama Ltd

The Grand Opening

With the contractor and the other various suppliers working flat out, the new railway was ready on time and the following notice appeared in the July 29th 1936 edition of the *East Kent Times*:-

---

Ramsgate Underground Railway
Opening on Friday

The opening of the Ramsgate underground railway by Mr. E. C. Cox CBE, traffic manager of the Southern Railway will take place at noon on Friday.

The railway, which will be electrically operated, runs from Hereson to Merrie England, joining up with the old steam train tunnel to the Harbour Station. The tunnel will be attractively decorated for 700 yards, providing a most unique ride.

The new railway will be opened to the public on Friday afternoon and there will be a regular service between Hereson-road and the sands.

The line duly opened on Friday, July 31st 1936, in time for the August Bank Holiday, and this special occasion was reported in the August 5th 1936 edition of the *East Kent Times* as follows:-

RAMSGATE'S NEW UNDERGROUND RAILWAY.
The Opening Ceremony. Remarkable Scenes.
S.R. TRAFFIC MANAGER AND THE TOWN'S PROGRESS.
1,000,000 Visitors in 1935.

Remarkable scenes marked the opening on Friday of Ramsgate's new underground railway, which connects the Dumpton area of the town with the Sands. The railway owes its inception to the enterprise of Mr.D.F.Warren, Managing Director of Ramsgate Olympia Ltd. (the proprietors of "Merrie England") and he and his business associates under the style of the Ramsgate Tunnel Railway Ltd., have established in the town something which is absolutely unique.

The railway, as has already been explained in these columns, starts from a station constructed at the eastern extremity of Bradshaw's Field, Hereson Road, Ramsgate, joins by way of a new tunnel with the original railway tunnel and ends at another station near the eastern end of the "Merrie England" site. It is no sense a "toy" railway, is run electrically and provides an almost direct connection between Dumpton Park Railway Station and Ramsgate's Sands.

In itself it represents a masterpiece of engineering for the whole of the work has been completed in one day less than twelve weeks in spite of innumerable technical and engineering difficulties. During that period the whole of the old railway tunnel in use has been cleaned, the new tunnel from Hereson has been driven, the track laid, the electrical power plant installed and the whole project put into running order.

So that the journey may be enlivened, the walls of the old tunnel have been embellished with scenic views of all parts of the world, so that it is possible to travel from Dumpton to the Sands via "Switzerland", "Canada", "Holland", "Japan" and "Egypt", while within a very few weeks other "countries" will be added to the itinerary.

The opening ceremony on Friday was performed by Mr.E.C.Cox, C.B.E., M.V.O., Traffic Manager of the Southern Railway Company, who during the course of his remarks, disclosed some remarkable figures and facts concerning the development of Ramsgate as a seaside resort. He said, among other things, that during 1935, the amazing total of 35,000 trains ran into Ramsgate Station bringing over 1,000,000 visitors to the town, and he admitted that one of the influences which compelled the railway company to abandon the old railway system in Thanet was Ramsgate's astonishing development as a seaside resort.

Those present at the opening ceremony which was conducted at the Hereson Road Station at Dumpton, included the Mayor and Mayoress (Alderman and Mrs.H.Stead) and most of the members of Ramsgate Town Council.

Introducing Mr. Cox to the assembly, Mr. Warren explained that the object of the railway was to facilitate transport for the public from the Southern Railway Station at Dumpton Park to the sands. When the tunnel was actually finished it would be completely decorated from one end to the other, but at the present time only six countries were represented in the scenic effects. When, however, those who were to make the first journey were translated into the land of "Make believe", they would be able to appreciate what the complete work would be like.

The trains used were an exact imitation of those used by the Southern Railway in their electric trains, with the exception of the bodywork of the coaches. The chassis, the bogie wheels and the brakes were miniature representations of those used by the Southern Railway electric trains. It was in no sense a "toy", it was a railway in the true sense of the word, except that it was smaller than most.

An interesting feature was that for the operation of the trains it had been possible to obtain the services of men who had been employed on the London Underground Railways, so that everyone who travelled on the line would have the satisfaction of knowing that the man in charge of the train was a man who had had many years' service and experience on the underground railway system of London.

Travelling Clock Souvenir

In conclusion, Mr. Warren said he believed that Mr. Cox was shortly to relinquish his position as traffic manager of the Southern Railway Company, and had chosen to spend his holiday by taking a trip to New Zealand and Australia. In view of this trip, Mr. Warren begged Mr. Cox to accept as a souvenir of the day a travelling clock.

After the presentation had been made, amid applause, Mr. Cox returned thanks, and then amid laughter, jocularly complained that after 50 years' association with railway work he had been invited to come to Ramsgate that day and "play at trains". From being traffic manager of the largest electric train service in the world, he found himself that day in the position of having been asked to open what was probably the smallest electric railway system in the world.

He could not help remembering the old railway tunnel. There were many people who despised the old tunnel and the old railway, but he was not one of them. The old railway served a very useful purpose in the early days when Ramsgate was smaller and offered fewer attractions to holiday-makers. After having served its purpose, it had to fade away out of existence.

Those who were resident in Ramsgate at the time would remember the very serious limitations presented by the old railway with the great growth of traffic which ensured consequent upon the increase in the population of the district. The tunnel was over a mile long and at the end there was a very short station, which made it very difficult to handle trains. Further, the gradient made it imperative that trains should stop in the tunnel to avoid running through the station on to the sea front (as in fact one did) and also the size of the turn-table made it impossible to use anything but short old-fashioned engines and therefore often two engines were required to haul a train out.

Re-Organised Railway System

The railway company fought against these limitations for years. To solve the problem they could not come further into the town and the only means of overcoming the many difficulties was to entirely re-organise the railway system of the Isle of Thanet.

This re-organisation had proved a great success and had helped the towns of the district, particularly Ramsgate, to push forward with their policy of attracting more and more people to the town. As a result of this, Ramsgate was becoming well known all over the country in the great industrial centres round London and even as far away as the midlands.

He went on to say that he would like to congratulate the originators of the present scheme for their great enterprise. They had carried out their project in the face of considerable opposition and one of those who had been opposed to it in its first inception had been himself. Now he wished to apologise to Mr. Warren for what he said to him when Mr. Warren called on him in 1933 when he came to interview the speaker with regard to a railway scheme in the district and went away disappointed.

Mr. Warren presented a scheme then which did not appeal to any of the responsible officials of the Southern Railway Company. They felt that the original scheme was impracticable and could not have been a success. It involved making another station between Ramsgate and Broadstairs, so that there would have been three railway stations on a mile of track and the whole thing would have been so costly that it could not possibly have been a sound proposition. It was with very great reluctance that he had to tell Mr. Warren that his 1933 scheme was impracticable.

He observed that in 1934 Mr. Warren approached the Ramsgate Council with a scheme, but again it was turned down, but now, in spite of all those difficulties, Mr. Warren had brought to fruition a scheme which the speaker felt would be of the greatest benefit to Ramsgate and would assist in attracting still more visitors to the town.

Ramsgate's Continued Prosperity

Before declaring the railway open, Mr. Cox congratulated those responsible for the government of Ramsgate for the successful manner in which they had carried out their policy of attracting more visitors to the town, and said it might interest his hearers to know that during 1935 no less than 35,000 trains brought over 1,000,000 people into Ramsgate. Therefore, it would be appreciated that the continued prosperity of Ramsgate was a matter of no small concern to the Southern Railway Company. Taking into consideration the spread of residential areas round London and the theory which had been freely advanced that industry in England was travelling south, he thought there was a great future in store for the district.

Following his speech, Mr. Cox formally declared the railway open and cut the ribbon barring the way to the station platforms.

Official visitors then made a journey by the first train to the Sands Station and returned.

Upon their return light refreshments were served, whereupon the Mayor proposed the toast of "The Tunnel Railway Ltd". In doing so, he said that Mr. Warren and his business associates had done much to put Ramsgate on the pathway to prosperity and the railway opened that day would certainly do much to add to the amenities of the town.

It was only appropriate, the Mayor said, that such an illustrious official of the Southern Railway Company as Mr. Cox should perform the ceremony of opening the line, because he could quite conceive that the Southern Railway Company bringing more and more people to Ramsgate. Visitors would now only have to cross the road and in a few minutes they could be transported to the sands.

Replying to the toast, Mr. Warren paid tribute to the various contractors whose intensive work had made it possible for the railway to be opened that day.

Mr.E.C.Cox cutting the ribbon and formally declaring the railway open.

East Kent Times

The report in the *East Kent Times* went on to say that the guests later adjourned to the Truro Court Hotel where luncheon was served in a marquee in the spacious grounds.

After luncheon the toast of "The Continued Progress of Ramsgate" was submitted by Sir Montague Hughman, the chairman of Holborn Construction Co. Ltd. The toast was replied to by Mr. Walter Daniel (president of the Ramsgate Chamber of Commerce and Advancement Association). Later, during his speech and amid laughter, Mr. Daniel congratulated Mr. Warren and his business associates on securing Bradshaw's field, which was something that everyone had failed to do in spite of all their efforts extending over a period of many years.

Alderman E.E.Dye, responded on behalf of the Corporation, and spoke of the advantage that private enterprise had over municipal undertakings.

The *East Kent Times* continued their report on this grand opening day as follows:-

Mr.D.A.I.Muntz, managing director of the Tunnel Railway Ltd., proposed "The consulting engineers, architect and contractor". He referred particularly to Mr. Greenly, the chief consulting engineer, and said that although there must have been times when, owing to various causes, Mr. Greenly must have thought there was very little hope of the railway ever being completed, he never failed to respond with enthusiasm to the demands made upon his time. He must also mention, he said, Mr. Martin, of the London Passenger Transport Board, who had also rendered valuable assistance as a consultant.

Speaking of the station at Hereson Road, Mr. Muntz said that it had been designed by Mr. Wood, of Messrs. Wood, Kendrick and Reynolds and built by Messrs. Darby and Martin of Ramsgate. Although the station was comparatively small, it was by no means easy to design, for owing to the limited space available and to the necessity of placing the building as near the Hereson Road as possible in order to maintain the correct gradient on the railway, it was a matter of working to inches and sometimes almost centimetres everywhere.

Mr. Alick Johnson, who was responsible for the scenic effects, and the Sign Construction Co., who flood-lit them, also deserved the best thanks of everyone for the manner in which they had carried out their respective jobs.

Mr. Muntz referred in terms of the highest oulogy to the work performed by the main contractors, the Holborn Construction Co., and their sub-contractors, the English Electric Co., who built the trains. It would be invidious to mention names of staff, but he thought he might be forgiven for mentioning Mr. Bill Cooper, the foreman of the works. Mr. Cooper was a great character and an amazingly efficient man at his job, and the speaker felt that the fact that the contract was completed on time was due in no small degree to his personal efforts. Responding, Mr.W.F.Bishop, director and general manager of the Holborn Construction Co. Ltd., said it was the exception rather than the rule for the contractors to be given a word of congratulations on the successful completion of a scheme, they usually had to content themselves with (to quote the words of the Mayor of Ramsgate a fortnight ago, when the new Winterstoke undercliff – also constructed by his company – was opened). "The satisfaction of a job well done".

When the contract was placed in the company's hands three months ago, it was realised that it would be only by thorough organisation and unstinted efforts by all concerned, that the job would be completed in time. Those efforts were put forward by his co-director, Mr. Colyer, by Mr. Maylett, of the head office of the company, by the local staff, by Mr. Muirhead, the local agent, by Bill Cooper and the able local labour which was engaged.

Over the August Bank Holiday, the new railway proved to be a great success and by the end of Monday (Bank Holiday) night carried some 20,000 passengers.

Passengers get ready to leave Hereson Road Station on the first train. Friday July 31st 1936.   Southern Railway Magazine

Another view of the opening celebrations at Hereson Road Station. Friday July 31st 1936. Pleasurama Ltd

Closed for the Second World War

With the new railway up and running, it was an immediate success and carried large numbers of passengers during its first short season which finished at the end of September. The line opened for the 1937, 1938 and 1939 seasons which was from Whitsun until the end of September.

Due to the outbreak of the Second World War, the line was closed and the whole of the main tunnel plus the recently bored narrow gauge tunnel became part of Ramsgate's most extensive network of deep air-raid shelters.

With war looking a strong possibility, the town's borough engineer and surveyor R.D.Brimmell had come up with a scheme in 1938 for tunneling galleries out of chalk. The only other similar known network of deep shelters was built in Barcelona for the Spanish Civil War.

Although the scheme at Ramsgate was twice turned down by the Home Office, it was finally given approval in 1939. By the time that the war had started, work was almost completed and with the inclusion of both the standard gauge and narrow gauge tunnels added to a further 3¼ miles of new tunnels, provided a semi-circular route of tunnels skirting the town with 18 entrances.

The contract for this work was awarded to Francois Cementation Co. Ltd., of Doncaster at a cost of £40,383 with an added £13,481 for seating, lighting, chemical toilets and the costs of converting the existing tunnels.

The first section of the new network to be opened was between West Harbour and Queen Street and was opened by the Duke of Kent on June 1st 1939.

With the Second World War approaching, the lone lady sits on the seat on the centre of the wooden platforms in this tranquil scene at Hereson Road Station in the late 1930's. A.W.Croughton

One famous wartime visitor to the shelter network was Prime Minister Winston Churchill who was on a special visit to Ramsgate when the sirens went off. He was quickly ushered to the Queen Street entrance.

After the war ended, the Tunnel Railway opened for the 1946 season although some of the illuminated tableaux needed replacing as the world views had been removed during the war.

A two car yellow train waits at the wooden platforms at Hereson Road. August 31st 1938. Arthur G. Wells

The original main tunnel in use as an air-raid shelter during the Second World War with the out of action narrow gauge railway track on the right of the photograph. Note the beds. Railway Magazine

Description of the Route

When opened, the line comprised of the single track 2ft gauge line branching into two platform tracks at each terminus with a passing loop in the tunnel about halfway along, which was equipped with spring points, protecting colour light signals and associated trip-cock mechanism.

The track was heavy flat-bottomed rail which was spiked direct to wooden sleepers. The lower terminus was known at various times as 'Sands', 'Beach' or 'Olympia' and comprised when opened of three wooden platforms serving the two tracks. This arrangement was for waiting passengers to board the trains from the centre platform, while arriving passengers left by the outer platform depending on which side the train arrived. T h e platforms and ticket kiosk were situated immediately outside the tunnel taking up very little space. In view of the colourful illuminated tableaux depicting scenes from various foreign locations on the wall of the original tunnel, the wording above the tunnel at the lower end said "WORLD SCENIC RAILWAY".

The lower terminus in its original form. The wording "WORLD SCENIC RAILWAY" can just be read above the tunnel. R.Shephard

Passengers waiting to board a train from the wooden platforms at the lower terminus. Author's Collection

The nameboard next to the lower terminus advertising the railway. R.Shephard

With no timetable, the trains service ran according to demand, when one train had a few passengers, the driver would signal to the other driver at the other station by means of a bell worked by a hand generator informing him that he was ready, and both trains would depart simultaneously to meet and pass at the halfway loop.

On leaving the lower terminus, the line became single and climbed a 1 in 75 gradient in the old tunnel for 780 yards where after passing the illuminated tableaux and the passing loop, branched left into the newer smaller tunnel where the gradient was at an average of 1 in 15. On arriving at the Hereson Road terminus, the trains completed their 1,144 yards journey in about 4½ minutes and had risen some 83 feet.

The station at Hereson Road was described as being near the Greyhound track and only 250 yards from Dumpton Park Station on the main line. The three wooden platform layout was similar to the lower terminus although on entering the station concourse, which was at street level, the three platforms were each reached by going down individual flights of wooden steps.

For many years, a familiar face at Hereson Road was that of ticket collector Tom Robson, who was thought to be a former Welsh miner.

By 1949, photographic evidence shows that the wooden platforms at Hereson Road were replaced by concrete.

In 1957, due to a collapse of part of the chalk cliff near the lower terminus, the railway remained closed while the cliff face was strengthened by means of a concrete wall, which meant reducing the lower terminus to a single track emerging from a small tunnel mouth and flanked with concrete platforms on each side. By this time, the world scenes in the tunnel had been removed and replaced by cartoon characters etc. The wording on the new concrete wall now saying simply "TUNNEL RAILWAY". The second track at Hereson Road was also lifted at this time.

As there was no depot provided on the line, trains were originally stabled at the lower end of the tunnel. This situation was changed in 1957, when a loop was added for this purpose at the same point in the tunnel using the track which was removed from both stations.

The entrance to Hereson Road Station. June 17th 1958.   H.C.Casserley

A two car yellow train at Hereson Road. April 19th 1949. Note the concrete platforms.

Arthur G. Wells

Looking down from the concourse at Hereson Road. June 17th 1958.

H.C.Casserley

A two car yellow train waits for passengers at the lower terminus. Note how the wording above the rebuilt tunnel entrance now reads "TUNNEL RAILWAY". September 9th 1964. H.C.Casserley

A two car red train waiting at Hereson Road. July 5th 1953.   John H. Meredith

Equipment and Operation

The English Electric Co., supplied the electrical sub-station which was located about 50 yards inside the tunnel at the lower end. The current supplied was at 400 volts and also installed was an associated A.C. switch pillar, liquid starter and a D.C. control panel. The sub-station consisted of a 150 h.p. three-phase, 410 volt, 50 cycle motor driving a 100 kw 400 volt generator. The D.C. supply was fed to the trains via tramway-type grooved overhead wire, supported on the walls of the old tunnel, by brackets in the roof of the new tunnel and on poles on the short open section at Hereson Road. The motor generator set was replaced by a small mercury arc rectifier of 460 volts in 1948.

The electrical equipment on each train consisted of two 30 h.p., 400 volts traction motors, totally enclosed and mounted over the driving axles of the power bogies. These bogies were quite heavy weighing approximately 7 tons which consisted of 5 tons bearing on the leading axle and 2 tons on the pony axle which also carried one end of the leading car. The non-driving axles were the ball and roller bearing type.

The drive from the motor to the driving axle was taken through single reduction spur gearing, the control gear being housed mainly in the adjacent driving compartment. Control was of the unit switch type with the entire operations centred on a single master controller.

Current collection was by means of a standard swivelling trolley with an English Electric sliding shoe. Braking was by means of a Westinghouse straight air brake arranged for both manual and emergency operation with a driver's brake valve in each driving compartment and emergency cocks distributed throughout the train. The air compressor for the braking system was motor-driven and was located in the driving compartment of each motor car. Hand braking was also provided and the driver's controls incorporated a 'dead-man's' handle.

Trains were provided with head and tail lamp fittings each with a clear and ruby bulb. Interior lighting for the cars was by means of 200 volt, 40 watt lamps arranged two in series and mounted in shallow rectangular fittings with chromium-plated rims and frosted glass panel dishes. The same fittings housed the emergency 6 volt 12 watt bulbs which were arranged for supply from a separate battery.

A two car yellow train at Hereson Road on a sunny day. June 12th 1964.　　　John H. Meredith

A two car yellow train at the Hereson Road Station platform waiting for more passengers before leaving for the lower terminus at the beach. July 25th 1964. Alan A. Jackson

The complete four car red train at the lower terminus. May 15th 1959. Arthur G. Wells

A two car yellow train approaching Hereson Road. June 22nd 1960.   Arthur G. Wells

A two car yellow train waits at the platform at Hereson Road. July 25th 1958.   Alan A. Jackson

Tickets

Tickets from the G.R.Croughton Collection

When the line opened in 1936, tickets for adults were 3d single and 6d return, while the fare for a child was 2d single and 4d return. These tickets, which were torn from a roll, were supplied by Williamson, Ticket Printers of Ashton. Over the years there was a very slight increase in price.

A two car yellow train at Hereson Road. September 9th 1964.   H.C.Casserley

The Final Season

After the line had re-opened in 1958 following the cliff fall near the lower terminus, the railway had continued running each season without incident. Unfortunately, on Thursday July 1st 1965 a descending train failed to stop at the lower terminus platform and crashed into the buffers. The *East Kent Times* reported this accident in their July 7th 1965 issue as follows:-

Driver trapped
CRASH ON THE TUNNEL RAIL

One of the Tunnel Railway trains carrying holiday makers to the sands at Ramsgate, on Thursday, failed to stop at the seafront station and smashed into the platform.

The front of the two-carriage electric train rode up over the platform and crashed into a building, completely wrecking the cab at the front and splintering the yellow carriages.

The driver, 74-year-old Mr. Ernest Brown, of 103 St. Lukes Avenue, Ramsgate, was trapped in the shattered cab. Visitors fought to free him and he was taken by ambulance to the Royal Sea Bathing Hospital with a suspected pelvic injury.

Holidaymakers who had travelled from Dumpton Park to the seafront through the tunnel were thrown about when the train ploughed into the platform.

One family of visitors, Mr. Henry Davenport, his wife and three daughters, Marilyn, Rose and Peggy of Biddulph House, Milne Estate, Woolwich, S.E.18, were all treated at the first aid hut for minor injuries.

Mrs. Ivy Bird, who has a shop next to the little station, was putting out postcards about 2.15 p.m. when the train ran into the buffers. "Instead of stopping it just sailed on", she said. "There was a flash and the cabin folded up like a concertina. It sounded like a plane crashing. A lump of wood flew across and just missed my head by a couple of inches".

The train ran several yards beyond the end of its rails and ended up in the wall of a staff toilet. Huge slabs of concrete forming the platform were cracked and the building was badly damaged.

"It was fortunate the building was there to stop it, otherwise it could have gone right through into the zoo", added Mrs. Bird.

One of the first rescue men on the scene was St. John Ambulance hut attendant Mr. George Pointer, who spent 39 years working on the railways.

Mr. Pointer, assisted by other men, helped the injured driver in his cab. "When I was on the railway I was trained for this sort of accident so I knew what to do", he said.

Investigation

Mr. Michael Allison, entertainments manager for Ramsgate Olympia Ltd., owners of the railway said the cause of the accident was not known.

He said the two miniature locomotives were checked very thoroughly.

(Left) The crash at the lower terminus. July 1st 1965. *(Right)* Close-up of the wrecked cab. East Kent Times

They had a maintenance staff who looked after them. "An inquiry will be held in co-operation with the local police", he said.

The driver, Mr. Brown, is a very experienced man. He had driven the train for a number of seasons and had made hundreds of arrivals at the station.

A retired handyman, Mr. Brown moved to Ramsgate with his wife from Beckenham.

The station was soon repaired and trains continued to operate for the rest of the 1965 season although the railway had for some while begun to have a "run down" appearance. The accident must have had an effect on the minds of the owners Ramsgate Olympia Ltd., who had recently changed their name to Pleasurama Ltd., and a decision was taken to close the line as the 1965 season finished.

With the general appearance of the railway beginning to look a bit "run down", a two car yellow train approaches Hereson Road. September 9th 1964.   H.C.Casserley

The end of the line at Hereson Road. September 9th 1964.   H.C.Casserley

After Closure

After the line closed, five of the original passenger cars went to the Hollycombe Steam Collection at Liphook in Hampshire where some were rebuilt on site. The other three cars went to the Hampshire Narrow Gauge Railway Society at Durley.

Some of the colour lights, rails, points and sleepers were sold to the Romney Hythe & Dymchurch Railway.

One of the passenger cars at Hollycombe in Hampshire on June 8th 1968.   John H. Meredith

The site of Hereson Road Station has been filled in and is now occupied by a petrol station while the upper and lower ends of the original LC&DR tunnel have been sealed up. The original tunnel and the narrow gauge tunnel are still intact and on special visits in August 1984 and January 1997, Subterranea Britannica, a society devoted to the study and investigation of man-made and man-used underground places, visited the site. Some of their interesting photographs taken by Nick Catford are shown here:-

The remains of a concrete platform at the lower terminus. August 1984.   Nick Catford

Looking north in the standard gauge tunnel with the narrow gauge tunnel to Hereson Road going off to the left. August 1984 . Nick Catford

The narrow gauge tunnel with a wall blocking the infilled area close to Hereson Road Station. August 1984. Nick Catford

The Tunnel Railway sign which was originally mounted on the south portal. January 1997. Nick Catford

Conclusion

Like many other unusual railways in the British Isles which have now vanished from our everyday scene, the Ramsgate Tunnel Railway will be remembered with much affection by local people, holidaymakers and railway enthusiasts alike.

The line was certainly unique and somewhat eccentric with not everyone liking the idea of travelling through an old sooty standard gauge tunnel and then a new much smaller tunnel which some people found a bit claustrophobic. However, the enterprise that was shown by Mr.D.F.Warren and his colleagues plus the connection of Henry Greenly as the consulting engineer certainly got the line off to a good start and perhaps the interruption of the Second World War took the momentum out of the venture. Even so, as a 2ft gauge passenger carrying electric railway running entirely underground, it still stands alone in the history of railways in Kent.

Acknowledgements

I would like to thank the following people and organisations for their kind help in compiling information and supplying photographs for this publication: Mr. Alan A.Jackson, Mr. Nick Catford, Mr. John H. Meredith, Mr. G. R. Croughton, Mr. R. Knight, Mr. D. E. Austen, Mr. G. Sutton and many other local people from the Ramsgate area, the National Newspaper Library at Colindale, the staff at Ashford Library, and last but certainly not least the following gentlemen who are unfortunately no longer with us:- Mr. J. L. Smith (of Lens of Sutton), Mr. H. C. Casserley, Mr. Arthur G. Wells, Mr. R. Shephard and Mr. D. Cullum.

My grateful thanks to Norman Branch for reading and checking my text and also to James Christian of Binfield Print & Design Ltd.

Bibliography

THE RAILWAYS OF SOUTHERN ENGLAND: INDEPENDENT AND LIGHT RAILWAYS by Edwin Course (Batsford)
THE RAMSGATE TUNNEL RAILWAY by Geoffrey Body & Robert L. Eastleigh (Published by Trans-Rail Publications)
THE RAMSGATE UNDERGROUND by Terry Wheeler (Published by the author)
THE RAILWAY MAGAZINE (Various issues)
THE RAILWAY WORLD (Various issues)
THE MODERN TRAMWAY (Various issues)

The sealed up tunnel at the site of the lower terminus. November 11th 2004.   Author